COMFORT ME WITH APPLES

Nell Leyshon

COMFORT ME WITH APPLES

OBERON BOOKS
LONDON

First published in 2005 by Oberon Books Ltd
521 Caledonian Road, London N7 9RH
Tel: +44 (0) 20 7607 3637 / Fax: +44 (0) 20 7607 3629
e-mail: info@oberonbooks.com
www.oberonbooks.com

A catalogue record for this book is available from the British
Library.

ISBN: 978-1-84002-633-7

Characters

IRENE
seventy, Roy and Brenda's mother

LEN
sixties, Irene's brother

ROY
forties, Irene's son

BRENDA
forties, Roy's twin sister

LINDA
forty

The play is set on a small dilapidated farm in a
village on the edge of the Somerset Levels.

This play was first performed on 20 October 2005 at Hampstead Theatre with the following cast:

IRENE, Anna Calder-Marshall

LEN, Alan Williams

ROY, Peter Hamilton Dyer

BRENDA, Helen Schlesinger

LINDA, Kate Lonergan

Director, Lucy Bailey

Designer, Mike Britton

Lighting Designer, Neil Austin

Music and Sound Designer, Nell Catchpole

Assistant Director, Dan Ayling

Costume Supervisor, Fiona Coutts

Voice and Dialect Coach, Jan Van Hool

Casting, Siobhan Bracke

Act One

Scene One

October. Dawn. The smell of cider apples fills the air: apples and oak and must and time.

The claustrophobic and dirty farmhouse kitchen. There has been a disturbance – chairs have been upturned, broken china lies on the floor. Behind the kitchen we see the vast orchard: a world of dying, falling leaves and over-ripe apples. Unpruned trees, falling trees, dead trees.

IRENE enters through the orchard. She is dressed in her winter nightdress, a cardigan over it. She wears Wellington boots, caked in fresh, red mud.

IRENE stands at the table and looks through the objects she has placed together: a pair of leather kneepads, a selection of grafting knives, a pair of glasses, an old notebook tied with string, a pipe. A large bundle of orange binder twine.

LEN enters from the house in his thick flannel pyjamas. IRENE watches as he walks round, looks for something, finds a packet of biscuits, carefully opens them and starts to eat. He looks at IRENE, sees her watching him.

IRENE: What you doing?

LEN: Nothing.

IRENE: Don't look like nothing.

> (*LEN walks to the table, rights one of the overturned chairs.*)
> (*Sharp.*) Don't touch it.
> (*LEN backs away. Eats another biscuit.*
> *IRENE picks up another chair and some broken china. LEN watches her.*)

LEN: Where you been?

IRENE: Out.

LEN: Cold, was it?

IRENE: No.

LEN: Oh.

> Warm, was it?

IRENE: No.

> (*Pause.*)

LEN: (*Careful.*) Reen. You all right?

(*No answer – IRENE continues to tidy. LEN steps forward to help, thinks again and backs off.*)

I said, you all right?

IRENE: What d'you reckon?

LEN: I don't reckon you are.

IRENE: Then why d'you ask?

LEN: Cos you're my sister.

IRENE: Am I? Well bugger me. Maybe you ain't so thick as I thought.

(*IRENE picks up and rights the last chair. She walks to the window, turns back, watches LEN eat another biscuit.*)

That your breakfast?

LEN: I like a biscuit.

IRENE: Do, do you?

LEN: I do, yeh.

Cold out, was it?

IRENE: Christ.

You already asked that.

LEN: Oh.

Where is it you been, then?

IRENE: To the orchard.

LEN: What were you doing out there?

(*No answer.*)

Must've been cold.

(*IRENE goes back to the table and fingers the objects again, places and replaces them. LEN watches.*)

Spec you keep thinking of what's happened.

Was a lot to take in, way Arthur went. I mean you think about it, one minute you're a wife, next minute you're a widow.

Ain't surprising you got so upset in the night. You know, all this. (*Gestures at room.*)

IRENE: You got anything important to say?

LEN: People do stuff when they're upset.

IRENE: Do they?

LEN: Don't even know what they do sometimes.

IRENE: No?

8

(*Pause. Then:*)

LEN: Took me a while to get back to sleep.

(*IRENE isn't really listening: she is looking at the items.*)

Yeh. Took a while. Lay in the dark and thought, will I ever get to sleep. Then as I was going off, I had that thing where you jump in the bed. Your heart goes like it's just woke up, then you can't get to sleep again.

You get to sleep, did you?

(*No answer.*)

Then, next thing I knew, it was morning, and the dark had woken me. Don't like a dark morning. Then I thought I heard summat down here. Thought I heard feet. So I come down and it was you. And here we are.

(*LEN walks to the window.*)

Got to be autumn out there. What with the apples.

(*Turns back.*)

Where's Roy?

He wasn't in his bed when I woke.

I thought, now where's Roy got to.

(*No response.*)

I can still smell the burning, Reen. From in the night.

IRENE: (*Sharp.*) Shut up.

LEN: I didn't mean nothing by it.

IRENE: I said shut up.

(*Silence.*

IRENE picks up the binder twine from the table, starts to untangle it, takes out one thread at a time and reties it.

LEN looks out the window again.)

LEN: Yeh. Trees is thick with apples.

Got to be autumn.

IRENE: You know it's bloody autumn.

(*LEN laughs.*)

LEN: Course I know it is. I was tricking you.

(*He eats another biscuit.*)

There is a lot of apples.

IRENE: There is, yeh.

(*LEN turns from the window.*)

LEN: Funny, how it gets dark come autumn.

Why's it do that, Reen?

9

IRENE: You know why.

LEN: Do I?

IRENE: Cos the days is shorter.

LEN: Why?

IRENE: Cos it gets dark earlier. Cos it gets light later.

LEN: But why?

IRENE: It's the sun and moon and that.

LEN: I don't like it dark.

IRENE: Some countries it's dark all day in winter.

LEN: I wouldn't like that.

You wouldn't think people'd wanna live there.

IRENE: Spec they was born there.

LEN: Spose.

IRENE: You get born somewhere, you wanna stay.

LEN: Yeh.

Thing about autumn is next thing you know, winter's here.

IRENE: Ain't a lot you can do about that.

LEN: I know.

Ain't just the dark I don't like. Don't like the cold neither.

IRENE: What do you like?

LEN: Biscuits.

(*LEN laughs at his own joke.*
LEN takes the binder twine from IRENE, tries to untangle it.
IRENE watches.)

Reen.

(*IRENE waits.*)

Did it hurt Arthur?

(*No answer.*)

Did he know, d'you reckon?

(*No answer. Then:*)

IRENE: When I went out, I stood in amongst the apple trees.
Just stood there.

LEN: Was you thinking of Arthur?

IRENE: No.

I was thinking back over the summer you was born.

LEN: Was you? Thinking of me?

You. Thinking of me.

IRENE: That summer I used to go to bed in the light. It was
hot and the window'd be open. I'd lay there and listen to
the men still working.
I'd look out and see the shape of her, you on her shoulder,
walking you up and down the yard, and you crying. You
used to cry all evening with the colic.
No one knew what to do with you.

LEN: I don't remember that.

IRENE: You wouldn't. You was a baby.

LEN: Don't remember Mother.

IRENE: I know.

LEN: D'you remember her?

(*No answer.*

IRENE takes the string from LEN, tries to untie it.)

IRENE: After Mother died we had to put you on the bottle
but you still cried and then it was me had to walk you up
and down.

LEN: Was I a good baby?

IRENE: You were all right. When you wasn't with the colic.

LEN: What would've happened if I hadn't had you to look
after me?

IRENE: Dunno.

LEN: Maybe I'd've gone in a home.

IRENE: Maybe.

(*IRENE loses her temper with the string, throws it to the
floor.*)

LEN: Reen. You all right?

IRENE: No.

LEN: Made it worse, no warning. Way it happened just like
that.

(*No response.*)

Didn't it?

(*No answer.*)

One minute he was all right, having a sit down, then he
was gone.

IRENE: (*Shouts.*) Shut up.

(*IRENE moves to the objects on the table, looks through them.
She takes an old, wooden, apple box and places the grafting
knives in it.*

11

LEN picks up the string again.

ROY enters quietly from outside, wearing an old overcoat. Boots caked in the same red mud.

IRENE leaves the box, steps forward, takes ROY's coat. LEN watches.)

IRENE: Been out?

(No response.)

Get any sleep?

(No response.)

Where you been?

ROY: *(Short.)* I said. Out.

IRENE: You never said.

Anyway I been out. Didn't see you out there.

(No response.)

Where were you?

(No answer.

(IRENE hangs up ROY's coat.

ROY looks out the window, his back to IRENE.)

You all right?

You angry, Roy?

(ROY turns.)

ROY: What d'you want me to say?

(ROY goes to walk across the kitchen, towards the door.)

IRENE: Where you going?

(IRENE deliberately picks up one of the grafting knives so that ROY sees it and stops.

IRENE takes the grafting knives out of the box, lays them out. ROY watches, and eventually:)

ROY: What you doing with his knives?

IRENE: Nothing.

ROY: You ain't getting rid of them?

IRENE: Would I?

(ROY touches one of the knives.

IRENE looks up at ROY.)

IRENE: You had any breakfast?

(No answer.)

Fancy a spot of bacon?

LEN: There ain't no bacon.

IRENE: (*Short.*) Always got bacon.

LEN: There ain't none.

IRENE: Day like today, got to have a cooked breakfast.

LEN: He can have some of these.

(*LEN holds out the packet of biscuits.*
IRENE snatches the packet off him.)

Re-en.

IRENE: Don't matter what you have, but Roy's a young man.
Got work to do.

LEN: What's there to do?

IRENE: Apples want bringing in. Press wants cleaning.
Lot to be done.

(*ROY picks up each of the knives, looks at them. IRENE*
watches him.)

(*To ROY.*) You get any sleep?

(*No answer.*)

Your bed warm enough?

LEN: Mine ain't warm enough.

IRENE: I'll get the eiderdowns out. Need summat heavy on
your legs come winter, pin you down.

LEN: I need a woman lie on top of me.

IRENE: What you say?

LEN: That's what people do come winter.

IRENE: Where d'you get that from?

LEN: You laid on Arthur, that's how you got the twins.

IRENE: Is it?

LEN: That's why women got two tits, case they have twins.

IRENE: So why's a cow got all they teats?

LEN: Cos it makes milking easier?

IRENE: So all them years ago they made cows so our
machines'd fit them easier?
Got a brain, have you?

LEN: Don't spose I ever thought about it.

IRENE: Ain't a lot you do think about.
Look at you, like an idiot. Close your mouth. Christ.

(*LEN throws the string down.*)

LEN: I ain't an idiot.

ROY: Course you ain't, Len.

(ROY takes his boots off.)

IRENE: Where you been, anyway?

(ROY shrugs.)

I said where you been?

ROY: Just out.

IRENE: You been bagging?

LEN: Apples he's been bagging.

IRENE: I'm asking Roy.

What apples? Royal Somerset?

LEN: Fair Maid of Taunton?

IRENE: Beauty of Bath?

LEN: Lambrook Pippin?

Kingston Black.

IRENE: Year you was born, Roy, trees was covered.

LEN: Good year for apples, good year for twins.

IRENE: Shut up.

LEN: Roy is a twin.

IRENE: I said you was an idiot.

LEN: I ain't said Brenda's name nor nothing.

ROY: Leave it, Len.

LEN: But I didn't.

IRENE: You idiot.

(IRENE moves towards LEN. ROY grabs her and pulls her back.)

ROY: Leave him.

(ROY lets go. IRENE brushes herself down.)

LEN: It's the shock.

ROY: I know.

LEN: She ain't herself.

ROY: No.

IRENE: I'm tired.

It was only yesterday.

(ROY stops.)

And I don't think I slept.

LEN: None of us got much sleep. All that upset in the night.

You and Roy and the shouting and that.

ROY: Leave it, Len.

LEN: Why?

(*No answer.*)

IRENE: (*To ROY.*) Is the vicar coming?

ROY: Yeh.

IRENE: Why's he coming?

ROY: Things to sort out.

IRENE: For the funeral.

ROY: That's it.

IRENE: Did I know the vicar was coming?

ROY: Course you did.

(*ROY walks towards the door.*)

IRENE: Where you going?

(*ROY turns back.*)

Roy. I keep thinking I can hear him. Talking and that.

Worrying about all the work there is to be done.

You reckon there's summat wrong with me?

ROY: You're all right. Don't start.

IRENE: What we gonna do without him?

Roy?

(*ROY stares at IRENE, places the box back on the table and gets a chair.*)

ROY: Here.

(*ROY places his hand on IRENE's shoulder, presses her gently down into the chair.*)

IRENE: Night I wed your father, he took an apple.

ROY: You said before.

IRENE: He cut it in half, and we ate one half between us
– put the other half under the bolster.

ROY: I know.

IRENE: (*Smiling.*) Yeh, one half under the bolster.

That was the night we wed.

(*Pause.*

ROY walks away.)

Roy. You reckon there's summat wrong with me?

ROY: No. Not that again.

IRENE: The apple left a stain on the pillowcase, I found it the next morning.

No matter how many times I washed it, it never came out.

ROY: I know.

(*ROY moves away.*)

IRENE: Don't leave me.

ROY: Len's here.

IRENE: But where you going?

ROY: I'm going for a piss. That all right?

IRENE: You go too often. Summat wrong with your bladder.
Always been weak.

ROY: Christ.

LEN: I'll stay here.
You hear that, Reen?
(*ROY leaves.*
Pause.)

LEN: You all right?

IRENE: No.

LEN: You really hear Arthur's voice?

IRENE: Yeh.

LEN: What's he say?

IRENE: Says there's apples all over the grass. Says there's
work to be done.
He's worried about what's gonna happen to us.

LEN: Oh.
Reen.
It's cold out.

IRENE: I know.
(*LEN walks round, looks out.*)

LEN: Like I said, I don't like autumn.
It's the dark evenings. And the leaves dying I don't like.
(*No response.*)
Reen.

IRENE: What?

LEN: We don't know what's gonna happen, do us?

IRENE: No.
(*Pause.*)

LEN: Reen.

IRENE: (*Impatient.*) What?

LEN: Do me the story of the orchard.

IRENE: I don't know it.

LEN: Course you do.

IRENE: I don't.

LEN: Reen.

> (*No response.*)

> You do.

IRENE: I know I do.

LEN: You tell it now, Reen?

IRENE: Not this morning.

LEN: Please, Reen.

IRENE: I can't remember it.

LEN: You can.

> One winter it was. In the beginning the ground was hard and it was dark.

IRENE: Was it?

LEN: Then was it the stars touched each other and made the light?

IRENE: Made the sun.

> (*IRENE goes to stand up. LEN pulls her back.*)

LEN: The man came. Reen. Please.

IRENE: Came out of the soil, the man, had the red of it on him.

> (*LEN claps his hands.*)

LEN: He did.

IRENE: He lay on the grass in the sun and his skin dried, and when he woke.

LEN: There was a woman.

> (*IRENE goes to stand up again.*)

> A woman, there was.

> And a tree grew.

IRENE: I'm tired.

> (*IRENE falls back in the chair.*)

LEN: And a tree grew. It did. It grew.

IRENE: I didn't get no sleep. I don't know.

LEN: There was leaves and blossom and fruit.

IRENE: There was apples.

LEN: Glory of the West,

> Silver Cup,

> King's Favourite,

> Cap of Liberty.

> (*Hesitates.*)

IRENE: Ten Commandments.

LEN: I know what he done with the apple. He picked it and ate it.

IRENE: He wiped it between the woman's legs first. Then ate it.

Her belly grew and one day her legs opened and the black branches of the Apple Tree Man came out of her.

LEN: Fell onto the grass.

And brought with them silver leaf, scab, mildew, clay-coloured weevil, apple twig cutter, honey fungus.

IRENE: Canker.

LEN: Codling moth, bitter pit.

IRENE: The Apple Tree Man built himself a room of trees and called it the orchard.

And he found the oldest tree and lived in it.

LEN: And that's where he lives now.

(*Pause.*)

IRENE: Like I say there ain't nothing wrong with me.

LEN: Course there ain't.

IRENE: Just don't reckon I got any sleep.

LEN: No.

(*Pause.*)

IRENE: You go and get Roy for me?

LEN: Why?

IRENE: I want him. Go on.

(*LEN leaves.*

IRENE stands up and walks to the table.

ROY enters.)

There you are.

Where you been?

ROY: You know where I was. What d'you want?

IRENE: I dunno what's gonna happen now.

ROY: No.

IRENE: Been a big shock. You got to know that.

ROY: Yeh.

IRENE: A person ain't herself when she gets a shock like that.

ROY: Ain't she?

IRENE: She ain't, no. Don't even know sometimes what she does.

ROY: What you trying to say?

IRENE: You know.

ROY: Do I?

> (*Pause.*
>
> *IRENE gestures at the box.*)

IRENE: I wouldn't get rid of his grafting knives. You know that.

> They're yours now.
>
> Roy.

ROY: What?

IRENE: This morning, before Len was up, I went out in the orchard.

ROY: I know.

IRENE: I was looking at the trees, thinking about your father. Course it was him planted a lot of them when he moved in. Grafted them too.

ROY: You told me.

IRENE: He'd say got to make enough cider for the workers, enough for us, and then a bit left to sell on.

> I was thinking about how when you was born that summer, how he knew he had someone to have the farm.
>
> (*IRENE watches ROY, seeing his reactions.*)
>
> How he always talked of when it's yours. How you'd look after it, how you'd know what to do with the orchard.
>
> Couldn't have this farm with no orchard.

ROY: But it ain't like that now.

IRENE: A son, he said when you was born. I got myself a son.

ROY: Did he?

IRENE: Yeh.

ROY: And Brenda? What about her?

IRENE: I'm talking about you, Roy.

ROY: Mother.

IRENE: No.

ROY: Christ.

> Look, I got to go.

IRENE: You can't go. Can't leave me here.

ROY: I got things I got to do.

IRENE: You got to see what it's like for me. Losing someone like that.

ROY: I know.

IRENE: Fifty odd years I had him. You imagine that.

ROY: Yeh.

IRENE: But he'd be all right, knowing you're here. Knowing you'll have it and it'll be looked after. And if I know he's all right, then I am.

You are here, aren't you?

(*No answer.*)

Roy.

I have got you here.

(*Hesitation.*)

ROY: You have, yeh.

(*Lights down.*)

Scene Two

(*Kitchen, as before. Later that morning.*

BRENDA enters. She looks round the room which she hasn't seen for three years. She walks to the table and sees the objects.

IRENE enters, still in her nightdress and boots. BRENDA backs away and watches as IRENE looks at the objects. IRENE looks up, sees BRENDA, and immediately conceals her emotions.)

BRENDA: Hello.

(*No answer.*)

You all right?

IRENE: Who let you in?

BRENDA: I did.

IRENE: What you doing here?

BRENDA: You know what I'm doing here.

IRENE: Do I?

(*IRENE walks away from the table.*)

BRENDA: Yeh. You do.

(*BRENDA goes to the table and looks through the objects, picks up her father's glasses. They are old, plastic, ingrained with his sweat and dirt.*

IRENE watches. BRENDA looks at her.

BRENDA places the glasses down and picks up the pipe.)

IRENE: (*Too loud.*) Don't touch that.
  (*BRENDA stares, places the pipe down.*
  Pause.)
BRENDA: Where's Roy?
  (*No answer.*)
  I said, where's Roy?
  Is he all right?
IRENE: Course he is.
  (*BRENDA turns back to the objects on the table, looks.*)
  Don't touch.
BRENDA: I'm not.
  (*Pause. BRENDA leaves the table, walks round the room.*
  Eventually:)
  When were you gonna tell me?
IRENE: Tell you what?
BRENDA: Why you doing this?
IRENE: You ain't making sense.
BRENDA: I am.
  (*Pause.*)
IRENE: How d'you find out?
  (*No answer.*
  IRENE realises:)
  Someone told you.
  (*Hesitation.*)
  Who was it?
BRENDA: God's sake.
  (*BRENDA walks away, gets control, turns back.*)
  Weren't you gonna tell me?
  (*No answer.*)
  Were you gonna leave it and in the end Roy'd have to tell
  me.
IRENE: So it wasn't Roy told you.
BRENDA: No.
IRENE: Who was it?
BRENDA: Does it matter who told me?
  Does it?
  (*Pause.*)
IRENE: So. What d'you come for, then?

BRENDA: What d'you think?

(*IRENE shrugs.*)

IRENE: We've managed these three years without you.

BRENDA: Three years? Didn't know you'd kept count.

IRENE: I didn't.

BRENDA: (*Laughs.*) No?

(*BRENDA looks round the room, at the state of it.*)

Was it sudden?

Was he ill before? Did you know it was gonna happen?

(*No answer.*)

Was it his heart?

It was, wasn't it?

IRENE: If you know, why you asking?

Well?

BRENDA: I want you to tell me.

(*IRENE fetches Arthur's suit on a hanger. Lies it across a chair, fetches a clothes brush from a drawer, starts to brush the suit. BRENDA looks at the glasses again, picks them up and smells them.*

BRENDA watches IRENE.)

BRENDA: Where is he?

IRENE: Who?

BRENDA: Dad.

(*IRENE busies herself, makes BRENDA wait.*)

I said, where is he.

IRENE: I know what you said.

They took him away.

BRENDA: When?

IRENE: Last night.

BRENDA: Where'd they take him?

(*No answer. BRENDA waits.*)

When's the funeral?

IRENE: When it is.

(*BRENDA looks round the kitchen, walks to the table and looks at the objects. IRENE concentrates on what she's doing, won't look up.*)

BRENDA: You getting any help?

IRENE: Why'd I need help? What you saying?

BRENDA: Doesn't matter.

(*Pause.*)

Mum.

Why didn't you tell me?

IRENE: Tell you what?

(*BRENDA slams down the leather kneepads on the table. IRENE stares then leaves the suit and, pushing BRENDA aside, rearranges the objects. BRENDA walks to the window, watches IRENE.*)

Know why I didn't tell you?

Didn't even think of you.

BRENDA: That's a lie.

IRENE: Didn't come into my mind. You never do. Not any more.

BRENDA: (*Laughs.*) That right?

IRENE: Yeh.

Someone said the other day, how's your daughter. I didn't know who they was talking about.

BRENDA: That right?

IRENE: That's right, yeh.

(*BRENDA starts to walk round, examines the kitchen. IRENE watches.*)

BRENDA: What did you say to them?

IRENE: I said, what daughter?

(*BRENDA opens a cupboard.*)

BRENDA: You said that?

IRENE: Yeh.

BRENDA: Even though you know it's three years since you saw me.

IRENE: I just guessed that.

BRENDA: Well it was a bloody good guess.

(*Pause.*)

D'you know when I last saw Dad?

(*IRENE looks up.*)

This year I saw him.

IRENE: You dunno what you're talking about.

BRENDA: I met him in town. In the bank.

IRENE: You never.

BRENDA: Maybe he didn't like to tell you.

IRENE: You're lying.

BRENDA: I'm not.

IRENE: Get out.

> (*IRENE goes to move towards BRENDA, who moves out of her way.*)

BRENDA: I ain't going nowhere.

> (*BRENDA gestures round the room.*)

Dunno what you been doing, look at this. State of the place.

IRENE: Fuck off.

BRENDA: Nice thing for a mother to say to her daughter under the circumstances.

IRENE: You ain't my daughter.

BRENDA: I am.

> (*Almost shouts.*) I bloody well am.

> (*LEN enters in his big coat and boots. He stops and stares at BRENDA. Takes his coat off and puts it on top of Arthur's suit. IRENE rushes to move it, and continues to clean the suit, and polish a pair of black shoes.*)

LEN: Is it you, Brend?

BRENDA: Course it is, Len.

LEN: You ain't been here for a long time.

BRENDA: I know.

How are you?

LEN: I'm all right.

IRENE: Got all day to stand and talk, have you?

LEN: No.

BRENDA: He's all right.

IRENE: Don't tell me if he's all right.

LEN: That Arthur's suit?

IRENE: It is.

LEN: Why d'you get that out?

IRENE: He's gonna be buried in it.

LEN: They bury you in a suit?

IRENE: They don't bury you naked.

LEN: Oh.

Brend. Where's Jack?

BRENDA: Outside in the car.

LEN: Oh. He's in the car.

　What car you got?

BRENDA: A red one.

LEN: What make, Brend?

BRENDA: Summat or other. Where's Roy?

LEN: Dunno. So Jack's outside in the car.

BRENDA: (*Starting to lose patience.*) Yeh.

LEN: It ain't a Land Rover?

BRENDA: It's a car.

LEN: Ain't never seen a red Land Rover. Seen green, brown.

　Ain't seen a red one.

BRENDA: No.

LEN: Is he coming in?

BRENDA: No.

LEN: Why's that, then?

IRENE: Cos he ain't.

BRENDA: Leave it, Len.

　(*Pause.*)

LEN: Arthur's dead.

BRENDA: I know. That's why I came round.

LEN: They took him away, put him in the car with the black
　windows.

　He's gonna be buried in his suit.

BRENDA: That's good.

　You all right?

LEN: Feeling sad.

BRENDA: That's how you're sposed to feel.

LEN: Is it?

　(*IRENE moves to her chair, sits and shines the shoes.*)

　(*To IRENE.*) You all right, Reen?

　(*To BRENDA.*) She didn't sleep.

BRENDA: Don't spec she did.

LEN: Up all night, she was.

BRENDA: Was she?

LEN: There were things happening here in the night.

IRENE: That's enough.

BRENDA: (*To LEN.*) Like what?

LEN: Nothing.

　So Jack ain't coming in.

BRENDA: No.

LEN: I'd like a go in his car.

BRENDA: I'm sure he'll take you one day. I'll ask him.

IRENE: You won't.

LEN: But I'd like that.

IRENE: (*To BRENDA.*) What you still here for? You been to see us. You can go now.

BRENDA: Can I?

Len, you do summat for me?

LEN: What?

BRENDA: You go and find Roy, tell him I'm here. Tell him I wanna see him.

LEN: Jack's in the car, you say.

BRENDA: Will you do that, find Roy?

LEN: Could be anywhere.

BRENDA: That's why I'm asking you, case you know places I don't.

LEN: Ain't nowhere here you don't know, you know it same as I do.

BRENDA: Please.

LEN: If you want. Only, I better put the coat back on.

BRENDA: You do that.

(*LEN puts his coat on.*)

LEN: I do the buttons when I'm outside. Depending. You know, on how cold it is.

BRENDA: Ain't too cold today.

LEN: How d'you know?

BRENDA: I just come here.

LEN: Oh.

See if I do the buttons up too tight, I can't breathe.

BRENDA: Leave it undone then.

LEN: But then the cold gets in.

BRENDA: Christ. You're going then, to find him?

LEN: Yeh. I'm to tell him you're here.

BRENDA: And that I wanna see him.

LEN: Right.

(*LEN leaves.*)

IRENE struggles to get up and BRENDA offers a hand. IRENE gestures her away, then manages to stand. She walks to the window.)

IRENE: I don't want you here.

BRENDA: (*Calm.*) I know. But I am here.

IRENE: I don't need you. Don't go thinking I need you.

BRENDA: Wasn't thinking nothing.

IRENE: I've managed fine without you.

(*Pause.*)

You met your father in town, you say.

BRENDA: Yeh.

IRENE: He told me everything.

BRENDA: He can't have done if he didn't say that.

IRENE: You're lying.

BRENDA: Am I?

(*Pause.*)

Where is Roy?

IRENE: Dunno.

BRENDA: Is he out?

IRENE: Might be.

BRENDA: What's he doing?

IRENE: What d'you do on a farm? He's working.

BRENDA: What work?

IRENE: There's a lot needs doing.

BRENDA: What like?

You seen the state of out there?

IRENE: Dunno what you're talking about.

BRENDA: No. Funny that.

Dad's gone now, you don't have to pretend it ain't like that.

How you managing for money?

IRENE: You better go now.

BRENDA: What's gonna happen here?

You even thought about it?

(*No answer.*)

You can't live like this.

IRENE: You saying it was summat here?

BRENDA: I'm saying you can't live like this.

IRENE: You're saying it was summat here caused it. When it was his heart getting worse.

BRENDA: Ah. So you knew he was ill.

IRENE: Where's Jack?

BRENDA: You could've told me and I could've come to see him.

IRENE: I said, where's Jack?

BRENDA: You know where he is. You heard.

IRENE: He ain't coming in.

BRENDA: Know what? He don't wanna come in.

IRENE: No need for him to come to the funeral either.

BRENDA: I know.

IRENE: No need for you to come.

(*No response.*)

Ain't gonna say nothing?

BRENDA: No.

(*Silence.*)

IRENE: That all you got to say, then?

BRENDA: What d'you want me to say?

IRENE: Nothing.

BRENDA: Fine. We won't say nothing then.

(*Silence.*

IRENE watches and BRENDA walks to the objects on the table.

Eventually:)

IRENE: What you doing?

(*No answer.*)

I said, what you doing?

BRENDA: Why you got these here?

(*No answer.*)

What you gonna do with them?

You getting rid of them?

(*No answer.*

BRENDA walks to the window, looks out.)

So he just fell down and died.

Did he know? Did he say anything?

(*No answer.*)

God's sake, what've I got to do, beg for you to tell me?

IRENE: He didn't know.

BRENDA: Did he ask for anyone?

Did he ask for me?

(*IRENE laughs.*)

IRENE: Why would he do that?

(*Pause. BRENDA controls her response.*)

BRENDA: Because I was his daughter?

IRENE: Never mentioned you when you was gone.

BRENDA: Only cos he knew he couldn't. Cos you wouldn't
let him.

IRENE: You wasn't never close.

BRENDA: No?

Thing is, you don't know. You don't know what we'd talk
about out there. You don't know everything. You think you
do but you don't.

You don't know how he'd tell me to take no notice of you.

IRENE: He never.

BRENDA: No?

All right, he never. That make you feel better?

(*No response.*)

So he didn't know, and he didn't say anything or ask for
anyone?

(*Hesitation, then:*)

IRENE: No.

(*IRENE walks towards the objects on the table.*

BRENDA watches her.

ROY walks in, speaking:)

ROY: He'll be here soon.

(*ROY sees BRENDA, stops.*

BRENDA stares at him.)

BRENDA: Roy.

(*ROY looks away, towards IRENE.*)

I sent Len out to find you, thought you were outside.

ROY: I was in there.

BRENDA: Been a long time.

IRENE: (*Quick.*) You finished the apples, have you?

ROY: What?

IRENE: Cleaned the press, have you?

ROY: Yeh. Yeh I have.

BRENDA: What's she saying?

ROY: Nothing.

BRENDA: Roy.

ROY: She's tired. She ain't slept.

(*To IRENE.*) You had anything to eat?

IRENE: No.

ROY: You want me to get you summat?

IRENE: No.

ROY: You gonna sit down?

IRENE: Don't think I slept.

ROY: No.

IRENE: It was the apples kept me awake. Heard them all
night, falling off the tree.

ROY: They're all gone now.

IRENE: Sounded like thunder, the weight of them falling.
You got the apples in, have you?

ROY: I have, yeh.

IRENE: There's someone here.

(*ROY looks towards BRENDA, looks away quickly.*)

ROY: She's all right.

IRENE: What's she doing here?

ROY: Come to see us.

IRENE: Why?

(*ROY takes IRENE's arm.*)

ROY: C'mon, Mother. Gonna go and lie down.

(*ROY leads IRENE off. IRENE looks back at BRENDA as
she leaves.*

*BRENDA looks round the room, then walks to the objects.
ROY returns.*)

BRENDA: What's going on?

ROY: She ain't been too good recent.

BRENDA: Never has.

ROY: Brend. She ain't been good.

BRENDA: I'm sure she ain't.

ROY: You heard her, talking like that. She's confused.

BRENDA: Is she?

ROY: Don't be hard on her.

BRENDA: Me, be hard on her?

ROY: It was only yesterday. She's shocked.

BRENDA: Len says she was up all night, says summat was going on.

ROY: He doesn't know what he's talking about.

BRENDA: Doesn't he?

ROY: No.

Look, God's sake, it was only yesterday.

BRENDA: Yeh.

I know.

(*Pause.*)

So. Was Father ill long?

ROY: Few months.

BRENDA: Had he seen the doctor?

ROY: No.

BRENDA: Why?

(*No answer.*)

Roy. Why didn't you tell me he was ill?

ROY: She didn't want me to say nothing.

BRENDA: Not to me, you mean.

Roy.

(*ROY doesn't look up.*)

How long were you gonna leave it before I knew he was dead?

ROY: I was gonna tell you.

BRENDA: When?

When?

(*No answer.*)

You know how I found out?

Linda told me.

(*ROY looks up quickly, meets BRENDA's eyes. Looks away.*)

She came to see me this morning, thought I knew.

First time I seen her in these three years and she had to tell me that my own father had died.

You know how that feels?

(*No response.*)

She told me you went to see her last night. After Father was taken away. Said you turned up, dressed in your suit.

Said you just sat there. Said it took her ages to get out of you what had happened.

Why didn't you come and see me?

ROY: I don't know.

I didn't think.

BRENDA: He was mine too, Roy.

(*Pause.*

ROY walks to the table, looks at the objects, walks to the window. BRENDA watches.)

BRENDA: Roy?

ROY: I don't wanna talk about it.

BRENDA: I'm sure you don't.

(*Pause.*)

When's the funeral?

(*ROY shrugs.*)

Lot to get done. There's people you got to contact. Have you spoken to the solicitor yet?

Roy.

Mother ain't gonna be up to doing it.

ROY: I know.

I'm gonna do it.

(*ROY looks out of the window.*)

BRENDA: You all right? You look like you lost weight.

ROY: I'm all right.

(*Pause.*)

BRENDA: What's gonna happen now? I mean here.

(*No answer.*)

State of the place shocked me. The yard and that.

Ain't nothing been done since I was here last.

Just falling apart.

(*ROY shrugs.*)

I heard the cattle'd gone.

ROY: Yeh.

BRENDA: So what's happening out there?

ROY: Nothing.

BRENDA: How you managing for money?

ROY: We ain't. We're living off the bank.

BRENDA: How long can you do that?

ROY: Long as they let us.

BRENDA: So what you gonna do? You can't keep this up.
I saw the orchard.

ROY: And? What's it matter?

BRENDA: State of it.

ROY: Didn't make any money anyway.

BRENDA: Ain't about money. You know that.

ROY: Well you ain't been here.

BRENDA: And you know why.
It shouldn't have been Linda who told me. You should
have come.
You should've told me.

ROY: I didn't know she was gonna come round.

BRENDA: When did you last see her?

ROY: Three years ago. Same as you.
(*Pause.*)

BRENDA: When you came in the room. You look more like
Father the older you get.
Can hardly look at you.
(*No response.*
IRENE returns, laughing, remembering something.
ROY walks towards her.)

ROY: What you doing? You was gonna lie down.

IRENE: Was I?

ROY: Yeh.

IRENE: I just remembered. The night Arthur wed me, he
picked an apple from the orchard. Cut it in two.
We ate one half, put the other one under the bolster for
after sex.

ROY: That's enough.

IRENE: I didn't sleep.
And now my legs is sore.

BRENDA: She got summat wrong with her legs?

ROY: They ain't sore. You're all right.

(IRENE pulls up her nightdress and touches her legs.)

IRENE: Look.

(BRENDA steps forward and IRENE pulls back.)

Mother's sent me to bed.

ROY: You ain't in bed.

IRENE: I'm in bed. My skin's raw.

ROY: You're in the kitchen with us.

BRENDA: She knows where she is.

IRENE: Where's everyone gone?

ROY: We're here.

(IRENE looks towards BRENDA, looks away.)

IRENE: I was in a tree. In the orchard. I was reaching out for an apple, and I fell.

I got blood on my legs.

(IRENE looks down and gestures.)

ROY: You ain't got no blood.

IRENE: I ain't?

ROY: There ain't nothing there.

IRENE: Oh. Good.

See, Mother said go playing with the Apple Tree Man, that's what you get.

I lay in bed and reckoned the Apple Tree Man was gonna smash the window, gonna come and get me between the thighs.

ROY: He ain't gonna do that.

IRENE: He ain't?

ROY: No.

IRENE: You promise?

ROY: Yeh.

IRENE: It ain't good for you, not getting any sleep.

ROY: No.

BRENDA: Maybe you better get some sleep then.

Maybe your little Roy better put you back to bed.

(IRENE stares at BRENDA.)

IRENE: Fuck off.

ROY: Brend.

IRENE: What you doing here?

BRENDA: You know what I'm doing here.

ROY: That's enough.

IRENE: What's going on?

ROY: It's all right.

IRENE: Where's Arthur?

BRENDA: You know where he is.

ROY: She's confused, Brend. Leave her alone.

BRENDA: Roy. She ain't.

ROY: It only happened last night.

BRENDA: (*Shouting.*) I know it only bloody happened last night.

IRENE: Tell her to get out.

(*ROY looks at BRENDA.*)

I said tell her to get out.

ROY: Brend. You got to go.

BRENDA: I done nothing wrong.

ROY: She ain't right.

IRENE: (*Shouts.*) Get out.

ROY: Go on.

(*BRENDA nods. Leaves.*
Silence.)

Scene Three

(*Kitchen, as before. Four days later.*
Morning. Autumn, and the smell of cider apples fills the air.
LINDA enters. She carries a bag, places it on the table.
LINDA looks round the room and remembers it from her last visit, over twenty years ago. She walks to the window and looks out over the orchard.
ROY enters carrying a heavy box which he places on the table. He looks at LINDA.
LINDA turns, sees ROY.)

LINDA: You can still smell the apples in the hall.

ROY: Never noticed.

LINDA: You're used to it.

Roy, you don't have to stare at me. You know what I look like.

ROY: Strange seeing you here again.

LINDA: (*Laughs.*) Anyone'd think you hadn't seen me for years.

ROY: I ain't.

LINDA: You saw me the other night when you came round.

ROY: Can hardly remember that.

LINDA: You were shocked. Shaking.

ROY: Was I?

LINDA: It's when someone dies that sudden. You got a job to take it in.

ROY: Spose, yeh.

Shaking, was I?

LINDA: A bit.

(*Pause.*)

I never told anyone before, but I used to pretend he was my dad.

He wasn't like mine, couldn't have been more different. After you came the other night and told me he'd died, I was thinking back, remembering how he'd take me out to where he'd put the chicken scraps on the roof of the shed. He'd watch me feed them and we'd just stand there. I'd hold his hand.

He never said anything, just let me hold him like that. (*Laughs.*) Then for a while I used to pretend I was yours and Brend's sister.

ROY: When?

LINDA: Only when I used to come to play. Before your mother threw me out.

ROY: That's a relief.

LINDA: What d'you think I am?

(*Pause.*)

He must have known what I was thinking. He knew my dad, knew what he was like with the drink and that. But he never seemed to mind.

(*LINDA looks round the room.*)

How is she?

ROY: What d'you reckon?
LINDA: Brenda says she's in her room most of the time.
ROY: She has been recent.
He always asked after you, when he had a chance.
LINDA: Did he?
ROY: Yeh.
LINDA: When she wasn't around, you mean?
ROY: He asked after you not that long ago.
LINDA: I don't believe you.
ROY: He did. Asked if I'd seen you these last three years. Since all that.
LINDA: What d'you say?
ROY: I said no. Told him you'd asked me not to come round any more.
(*LINDA nods.*)
You don't know what it's been like.
LINDA: Roy. I asked you not to say anything.
ROY: I know. I didn't mean to.
LINDA: I knew I shouldn't have come in.
(*LINDA takes a step towards the door. ROY blocks her.*)
ROY: Don't.
LINDA: Roy.
ROY: I know. I'm sorry. I won't say nothing.
LINDA: I've made a mistake.
ROY: No. It's my fault.
LINDA: What time's the funeral?
ROY: Four o'clock.
LINDA: I'm not sure I should go.
ROY: Why?
LINDA: It's all so bloody difficult.
I don't want to make it any worse.
ROY: But you said you'd come. You said you wanted to.
LINDA: I do.
ROY: I didn't mean to say anything.
LINDA: Then don't.
ROY: It ain't easy.
LINDA: If you say anything I'll go.
(*LINDA looks around.*)
There's so much changed.

ROY: Been a long time.

LINDA: Brend said the cattle're gone.

ROY: Went a while ago.

LINDA: You growing anything?

ROY: No money in it.

LINDA: And the orchard?

ROY: Still there.

LINDA: Roy.

ROY: I know the place is a state.

LINDA: It's been let go.

ROY: That's what happens when you don't work it. Don't take long to get like this.

LINDA: So what are you doing?

(*ROY shrugs.*)

How d'you fill your days?

ROY: I wait.

LINDA: What you waiting for, Roy?

(*ROY shrugs.*)

You thinking if you don't do nothing, something'll happen in the end?

ROY: Maybe.

LINDA: (*Angry.*) For God's sake.

Ain't you learned anything? You seen what happens when you wait and do nothing.

This is what bloody happens. Us being here, like this.

(*ROY looks away.*

LINDA walks away, calms herself, turns to the box, starts unpacking. ROY watches.

LINDA stops. Sees ROY looking at her.)

LINDA: I'd better go and help Brenda.

ROY: (*Quick.*) No. She'll be all right.

(*LINDA unpacks, then sees ROY is still staring at her.*)

LINDA: Please don't.

(*ROY still stares.*)

Roy. Don't.

(*LINDA takes a step towards the door.*)

ROY: Don't go.

(*ROY stops her, holds her arms.*)

LINDA: Let me go.

ROY: No.

LINDA: You have to let me go.

(*ROY tries to kiss LINDA.*
LINDA shakes him off.)

You can't.

(*ROY clears his throat, tries to speak.*)

ROY: Linda.

LINDA: Don't.

(*LINDA moves towards the door, ROY follows.*)

ROY: Listen to me.

LINDA: No, Roy. Don't say it. Please.

ROY: Why?

LINDA: I didn't come for this. Please.

(*BRENDA enters, carrying another bag. She sees them, stops.*)

Is that everything?

BRENDA: Yeh.

(*BRENDA takes the bag to the table.*)

I was talking to Len.

LINDA: I was just going.

BRENDA: Don't rush off.

LINDA: I got things to do.

BRENDA: Funny seeing you here again.

LINDA: That's what Roy said.

BRENDA: Wish Dad could see you back here.

LINDA: We were just talking about him.

BRENDA: Were you?

LINDA: I told Roy, how after school he'd have the chicken scraps ready.

BRENDA: He loved it when you came round.

LINDA: Not as much as I did.

BRENDA: We never wanted you to go home. Did we, Roy?

(*ROY looks away.*)

Mind, there was the time Dad gave you the first taste of the cider. Roy never got over that. (*To ROY.*) Did you? He was furious.

LINDA: I was the youngest.

BRENDA: But Roy'd always had it. Didn't you?

LINDA: You still got the press?

BRENDA: It's still there, yeh. Somewhere under the junk out
there.

(BRENDA starts unpacking the bag.

LINDA watches BRENDA as ROY watches LINDA.)

Thanks for helping.

LINDA: Brenda.

I'm not sure about coming to the church.

BRENDA: Course you're coming.

LINDA: It'll make it so difficult.

BRENDA: It already is difficult.

Roy's got to tell Mother, ain't you, Roy? Just say Linda's
coming and that's the end of it.

*(ROY watches LINDA, who moves back to the window and
looks out.*

BRENDA sees LINDA looking out.)

Lot of apples this year. It was the mild spring, wasn't it,
Roy?

LINDA: Spec it was Roy singing to the trees.

BRENDA: *(Sings.)* Hatfuls, capfuls.

LINDA: *(Sings.)* And a little heap under the stair.

BRENDA: Haven't sung that for a bit.

LINDA: No. Did you hit the trees with the stick, Roy?

ROY: Not last year.

LINDA: Did you believe it worked?

ROY: Yeh.

LINDA: I did, too.

BRENDA: So what's it like being back? Got to be well over
twenty years.

LINDA: Yeh. Feels odd.

I couldn't believe it when she said I couldn't come back.

BRENDA: Don't reckon we could. Could we?

(BRENDA looks at ROY but he stares at LINDA still.)

LINDA: I ought to get going.

(LINDA moves.)

BRENDA: Why?

LINDA: I said I'd be somewhere.

BRENDA: Oh.

You still managed to see each other though. (*Laughs.*) The lies I told. Sometimes when she asked where he was, I didn't know if he was with you so I told a lie anyway. He was probably out milking.

LINDA: Please, Brenda.

BRENDA: What?

LINDA: I said I got to get going.

BRENDA: Course. Sorry.

You are coming to church, aren't you?

LINDA: I don't know.

BRENDA: You got to. We want you to. Don't we, Roy?

(*No response.*)

Roy.

ROY: Yeh.

LINDA: I'll think about it. I'd like to, but –

BRENDA: Just come. It'll be fine.

LINDA: Maybe.

BRENDA: Thanks for the lift.

LINDA: That's all right. I'll get going then.

BRENDA: All right. See you there.

LINDA: Bye, Roy.

ROY: Yeh. See you.

(*ROY watches her as she leaves.*

BRENDA looks up and sees ROY looking after LINDA.)

BRENDA: Good to see her, ain't it? I mean back here at home.

She don't seem to get any older, I swear I'd seen her the other day, not three years ago.

(*No response.*)

You all right?

ROY: Yeh.

BRENDA: You gonna give us a hand?

Take that end.

(*They move the table and chairs.*)

Bit more. There. That's better.

Yeh. Felt right, her being here didn't it?

ROY: Leave it.

BRENDA: Why?

ROY: I said. Leave it.

(*BRENDA shrugs, moves the things on the table.*)

BRENDA: Jack said to say hello. I can say that, can I?

ROY: Don't be stupid.

BRENDA: I ain't being stupid.

ROY: You are.

BRENDA: Jack said he could see the problem here. You know, the debts and that. And you stuck here. You know he could help.

ROY: Look, there ain't no bloody problem. All right?

(*BRENDA laughs.*)

BRENDA: Course there ain't.

ROY: Why you laughing?

Don't laugh.

BRENDA: Jesus, Roy.

All right. Let's start again.

Hello, Roy. D'you wanna give me a hand in with this stuff.

ROY: You're really being stupid now.

BRENDA: Am I?

ROY: You know you are.

BRENDA: There ain't nothing I can say. Can't talk about Linda.

(*Hesitates.*)

Can I?

ROY: No.

BRENDA: Why?

ROY: Christ, Brend. Don't start.

BRENDA: I ain't starting up.

ROY: No?

BRENDA: No.

Roy.

ROY: What?

BRENDA: I know the bank's asking to see you. What if they call in the loans?

(*ROY gestures at the table.*)

ROY: Let's just get this done, eh?

BRENDA: Roy.

Mother and Len, they ain't up to sorting this out. You got to take control.

ROY: Have I now?

BRENDA: I know you all been living like this for Father's sake. But he's gone now.

You can say it now. There's nothing going on out there. Is there?

(*ROY shrugs.*)

You reckon it'll make her happy? Keeping your head down and doing nothing?

You know the bank won't let it stay like this for ever, even if you will. They'll take it and it'll all be too late.

You ain't even listening, are you?

ROY: I am.

BRENDA: What did I say then?

ROY: You know what you said.

BRENDA: Christ, Roy. You reckon you got forever to do something?

ROY: No.

BRENDA: Well you could've bloody fooled me.

So what are you gonna do?

(*Long, long pause.*

BRENDA moves towards door.)

ROY: Where you going?

BRENDA: Out for some bloody air. I can't breathe in here.

(*BRENDA leaves.*

Lights down.)

Act Two

October. The smell of cider apples fills the air.

The vast orchard in late afternoon, following the funeral. A world of dying, falling leaves and over-ripe apples. Unpruned trees, falling trees, dead trees.

The light fades slowly through sunset to dark during the act.

In the orchard, there are hessian bags full of apples leaning against the trees. Empty bags on the ground.

A spade stands in the earth where an attempt has been made to dig a hole.

IRENE wears her black dress, a coat on top. She wears her Wellington boots. She tries to dig. By her feet lie the grafting knives.

LEN arrives in the orchard. He wears a black three-piece suit, black tie, boots. He watches IRENE dig.

LEN: What you doing?

    (*No answer.*)

    What's that for?

    (*No answer.*)

    I said what d'you wanna do that for?

IRENE: I can't lift it.

LEN: Here.

    (*LEN takes the spade.*)

    Earth's heavy, that's why you can't lift it. How deep's it gotta be?

IRENE: Not too deep.

    (*LEN cuts a square, lifts a sod of grass and earth.*)

LEN: What's it for?

IRENE: I knew before.

LEN: You forgot?

IRENE: Forgot, yeh.

    (*LEN stops.*)

LEN: You all right?

IRENE: I'm all right. Just come out here for a bit of air. You need a bit of air, time like this.

LEN: Brenda told me to come and get you, told me to tell you there's a tea ready.

IRENE: Did, did she?

LEN: Yeh.

> (*Waits.*)

> They're all waiting for you.

IRENE: I spec they are. That's why I'm out here, Len.

LEN: Oh.

> (*IRENE leans back against a tree, looks up at the sky.*
> *LEN begins to dig again, stops, looks up where IRENE is*
> *looking.*)

> What you doing now?

> (*No answer.*
> *LEN looks up at the sky.*)

> What you looking at?

> (*No answer.*)

> You ever seen a shooting star?

IRENE: Yeh.

LEN: I haven't.

IRENE: You have.

LEN: How?

IRENE: Father showed us.

LEN: When?

IRENE: Brought us out here and we looked at them.

LEN: Well I'll be buggered. Don't remember that.

IRENE: They ain't stars, anyway.

LEN: Oh.

> So what are they then?

IRENE: They're bits of dust or rock and that.

LEN: Oh.

> (*LEN digs again, stops, remembers.*)

> See, reason I ask is I heard this thing.

IRENE: What's that?

LEN: I heard this woman down on the moors was hit by a
shooting star. They reckon it came right through the roof of
her house and hit her on the hip.

IRENE: On the hip?

LEN: That's what they say.

IRENE: How's it gonna get her on the hip?

LEN: I wondered that.

45

IRENE: I mean if it's coming from up there, how's it gonna get your hip. Less she was lying down in bed on her side.

LEN: She could've been.

IRENE: But you'd have thought she'd've had time to move.

LEN: I'm only saying what I heard.

IRENE: Well they must make some noise. Would've been right by her head. I mean you'd hear that, know summat was up, and you'd move. I mean you wouldn't just lay there waiting for it to come, exposing your hip like that. Don't make sense.

LEN: Oh.

IRENE: Can't be right, your story.

LEN: Like I said, I'm only saying what I heard.

IRENE: Reckon you got confused. Wouldn't be the first time.

LEN: All right. Don't go on.

IRENE: I ain't going on. Just saying. Just getting it clear.

LEN: Well not everything's clear.

IRENE: Not in your bloody world, no.

(*Pause.*)

LEN: It don't feel the same. With Arthur here, it all felt real.

IRENE: Well he ain't here.

LEN: (*Strong.*) I know he ain't.

(*LEN looks up, examines the sky for a few moments.*)

IRENE: What you looking at?

LEN: I know what they say about the earth and moon and sun and that. That they all go round separate, but it don't seem like it.

The sky looks like it joins them all up.

IRENE: It don't. It's just air.

LEN: But if we're going round like that, not joined up, anything could happen.

We could fall.

IRENE: Reckon we have fallen.

(*IRENE takes one of the grafting knives and begins to peel an apple; the length of peel falls to the ground.*
LEN watches.)

LEN: We going in?

(*No response.*)

It's getting colder.

(*No response.*)

And darker.

IRENE: Is it?

LEN: It is, yeh.

You cold?

(*No answer.*

LEN takes some of the peel.)

What's that? Morgan Sweet?

(*He bites.*)

IRENE: Ashton Bitter.

(*LEN spits the sour apple out. IRENE laughs, continues to peel.*)

LEN: You ever think about me?

IRENE: Why d'you ask that?

LEN: Cos that morning, after Arthur went, and you was out in the orchard, you said you was thinking about me.

IRENE: Did I?

LEN: That's what you said.

IRENE: What's got in you today?

LEN: Been a queer day.

(*LEN watches IRENE.*)

Why you staying out here, Reen?

IRENE: Nowhere else I wanna be.

LEN: It put you in mind of Arthur?

(*IRENE steps away, looks round the orchard.*)

IRENE: Puts me in mind of everything. There ain't nothing without this.

LEN: Ain't what it was.

IRENE: Don't say that.

After Mother died, that autumn, I helped Father get the apples in. You was in the old pram out here, under the tree. You'd watch the branches and leaves.

LEN: Ain't a lot changed then.

IRENE: You ain't in the pram.

LEN: Would be if we had one big enough. I'd like that, sat there just looking. Nice blanket to thread the fingers through.

IRENE: Daft old thing.

LEN: I am a daft old thing, yeh. I am.

IRENE: Day I helped get the apples in, Father said to leave the last one on the tallest tree. For the spirit. Said it'd come for it in the night.

So I got out of bed, come out and waited. Stood here for ages but it was the first frost and I got cold so I went on in.

LEN: What happened?

IRENE: I went out early next morning, but the apple'd gone.

LEN: Where was I?

IRENE: You was in my bed. Where you slept.

Father'd pushed it against the wall and nailed a board alongside so you wouldn't fall out. When I got back in the bed I put my feet on you to warm them. You always had that hot skin.

LEN: How hot was I?

IRENE: Hot.

LEN: Was I dreaming when you come in?

IRENE: How'd I know what was in your head?

LEN: Do babies dream?

IRENE: Must do.

LEN: Was I a good baby?

IRENE: You was, yeh.

LEN: You never minded looking after me?

IRENE: Didn't have no choice. Just got on with it.

Always had men to look after. Had to look out for Father when Mother was gone. And I had you to mind. Then I got wed and I had Arthur.

And then a few years later I had Roy.

LEN: What about Brenda?

IRENE: Did I say I had men to look after?

LEN: That's what you said, yeh.

IRENE: I didn't mean to say that.

LEN: Cos of Brend.

IRENE: No.

Cos you ain't a man.

LEN: I am.

IRENE: Not like a man should be.

LEN: Why d'you say that?

   (*No answer.*)

   I don't like it when you're like that.

IRENE: I know.

LEN: You don't wanna go getting like that.

IRENE: Why?

LEN: Cos you get yourself upset, like the night Arthur died
   and you did that to Roy.

IRENE: Did what?

LEN: You know what.

IRENE: I didn't do nothing. You hear. Nothing.

LEN: See, you're getting upset again.

IRENE: Ain't bloody surprising, seeing as what a day I've
   had.

LEN: No.

   We ought to get on in.

IRENE: I ain't going in.

LEN: But it's gonna get dark. You know I don't like the dark.

IRENE: Don't you?

LEN: Don't like winter. Don't like the bare branches.

   (*Silence.*)

   Reen. What's gonna happen?

IRENE: With what?

LEN: With everything.

   (*No answer.*)

   We will be all right, won't we?

IRENE: What d'you want me to say?

LEN: That we'll be all right.

IRENE: Do you?

LEN: Say it.

   Please.

IRENE: No.

   (*Pause.*
   LEN takes the spade and digs more.
   IRENE sorts the knives.
   ROY enters the orchard and approaches. He wears an ill-fitting
   suit from the 1950s.
   IRENE watches.)

   He looks like his father.

LEN: He's younger than Arthur.

IRENE: Christ. Course he bloody is. What is it you got between your ears?

LEN: Don't be like that again.

ROY: Leave him alone.

IRENE: No.

ROY: Take no notice, Len.

LEN: I can't do that.

IRENE: Ain't a lot you can do.

ROY: Stop it. I said leave him alone.

IRENE: He can go in now, anyway.

LEN: Ain't going in without you.

(*To ROY.*) I told her to come in. She wouldn't.

IRENE: I won't. Not while that woman's there.

ROY: What woman's that?

IRENE: That one.

House full of bloody women.

ROY: Don't bloody start up.

IRENE: She still there?

ROY: Linda, her name is. Linda. She's been helping Brend. They're trying to help.

IRENE: I don't need no help.

Tell them to go.

ROY: No.

IRENE: (*Loud.*) I said tell them to go.

ROY: (*Shouts.*) No.

I said don't start again.

IRENE: I ain't starting nothing.

LEN: (*Shouting.*) Stop it.

IRENE: (*To LEN.*)You shouted at me.

Day like today, and you shouted at me.

LEN: I never shouted.

IRENE: You did.

LEN: It was Roy shouted.

ROY: Leave it, Len.

IRENE: What's happening, Roy? Why you shouting at me?

ROY: I ain't shouting.

IRENE: You was. What's happened with you? Why you being like this?

ROY: I ain't being nothing.

IRENE: What's on? I know summat's on.

ROY: Ain't nothing on.

IRENE: Ain't been an easy day for me.

ROY: No. I know.

IRENE: I feel weak.

ROY: Come on. Let's get you in.

IRENE: We can't go in. We got all this out here to do.

ROY: What we got to do?

IRENE: All this.

(*ROY waits.*)

There's all the apples to bag.

ROY: We don't have to do it all today.

IRENE: And there's the trees.

ROY: What about them?

IRENE: They're gonna want pruning. But only Arthur knew how to prune a tree.

LEN: Ain't difficult, prune a tree.

IRENE: He knew how to let the light in.

LEN: Me and Roy can do it. We'll get the saw out, cut a few branches. And I can paint the tar on, stop the bleeding. Can't us, Roy?

(*No response.*)

We'll beat the branches. The birds'll fly off and we'll sing to the trees.

(*Sings.*) Oh apple tree, we'll wassail thee

For the Lord does know where we may go

To be merry another year.

IRENE: You can't sing.

LEN: I can.

IRENE: You got a horrible voice.

LEN: That ain't nice.

ROY: Leave him alone, Mother.

IRENE: Don't start on me again.

ROY: I ain't.

IRENE: You know you are.

ROY: Come on. Let's go in.

IRENE: We can't leave it like this.

ROY: But it's been like this a while now.

IRENE: We gotta get it done. Or I'll start hearing his voice,
he'll be saying to me, Reen, you got to get that work done.
What you doing with it all?

ROY: He ain't talking to you. It's just in your mind.

IRENE: But I can hear it.

ROY: You think you can.

IRENE: I can.

ROY: (*Gentle.*) You can't.

Come on, you know we ain't been working out here for
years. Look at it. Look at the trees.

(*IRENE refuses to look.*)

They look pruned to you?

Look at them.

IRENE: You don't know what you're talking about.

(*ROY picks up one of the knives.*)

ROY: When was this last used?

IRENE: What you trying to say to me?

(*IRENE takes the knife from ROY and places it back with the
others.*)

I couldn't sleep last night. I was lying there thinking about
today. Thought I could hear the men talking in the yard.
Hear the wagons bringing in the apples.

LEN: You must've been dreaming.

IRENE: I could feel a weight on the mattress. I could hear
your father's voice. He was talking to me, telling me what I
had to get done.

His voice in my head.

It's only when you're here it stops.

(*ROY picks up an apple. IRENE takes it off him.*)

IRENE: You hear that?

ROY: I heard it, yeh.

(*IRENE touches ROY's suit, then brushes it, adjusts it on the
shoulders.*

*BRENDA enters the orchard and when ROY sees her, he takes
a step away from IRENE, tries to keep a distance.*)

BRENDA: I didn't know where you were.

LEN: She wouldn't come in.

BRENDA: Doesn't matter.

LEN: It does, Brend. I was worried all they sausage rolls'd be gone.

BRENDA: I've kept you some for later.

(*LEN rubs his hands together.*)

LEN: I like pastry.

BRENDA: I know.

LEN: I like meat too.

BRENDA: I know.

LEN: Like lots of things.

BRENDA: You do, yeh.

LEN: You always been good to me.

BRENDA: I try, Len.

(*To IRENE.*) Mother.

(*IRENE ignores her.*)

You all right out here?

Come out for some peace, did you?

Don't pretend you can't hear me.

IRENE: What's that noise, Len?

LEN: What noise?

IRENE: Like someone talking.

LEN: It's Brenda.

(*ROY turns back, gets drawn in again.*)

ROY: (*To IRENE.*) Stop it. Don't do that.

IRENE: Well. She still here?

BRENDA: Don't do this to me. Not today.

ROY: Leave her alone.

IRENE: Why?

ROY: Cos I'm asking you to.

(*IRENE is silent.*

BRENDA looks round.)

BRENDA: I ain't been out here for a long time.

LEN: Ain't you?

BRENDA: No.

LEN: No. Don't spose you have.

BRENDA: Christ, the hours we'd be here, eh?

LEN: You two buggers'd never come in.

BRENDA: We used to hear you shout for us, and we'd climb higher in the trees. Watch you looking for us.

LEN: And you was in the trees?

BRENDA: Watching you, yeh.

LEN: Buggers.

Reen'd be shouting at me, and I'd be looking for you.

Arthur'd be threatening the belt when you was found.

Buggers, you were. Buggers.

BRENDA: You loved us being here.

LEN: I did.

BRENDA: We had to run away to stop you joining in the games.

LEN: (*Laughs.*) Yeh.

Arthur'd be telling me to get on with the day's work. He'd say let the twins alone, let them play in bloody peace.

(*Pause.*)

BRENDA: He never used the belt.

LEN: Course he never.

BRENDA: He'd never do that.

LEN: Too soft for that.

BRENDA: Too soft for life really.

IRENE: What you trying to say?

ROY: She ain't trying to say nothing.

IRENE: You're trying to say summat about the way he was.

BRENDA: He was what he was to me. You ain't changing the way I see things.

ROY: Leave it, Brend.

BRENDA: Yeh.

(*Pause.*)

The hours we spent out here.

ROY: Yeh.

BRENDA: All these trees fallen.

IRENE: They ain't fallen.

BRENDA: I don't like to see it like this.

ROY: I know.

IRENE: (*Quick.*) Like what?

BRENDA: Grown over.

IRENE: Ain't grown over.

BRENDA: You only got to leave it a while and it all goes.

IRENE: You don't know what you're talking about. Just needs a bit of work. That's all.

ROY: Christ.

(*ROY starts to unbutton his jacket.*)

IRENE: What you doing?

BRENDA: What d'you think he's doing?

IRENE: Why you doing that?

ROY: It's too tight.

IRENE: It was good enough for your father to marry in.

BRENDA: Leave him alone.

IRENE: No.

LEN: Thing is, Reen burned his suit. That's why he's got this one on.

IRENE: (*Sharp.*) Shut up.

BRENDA: What you saying?

IRENE: He don't know what he's saying.

(*LEN looks away.*)

BRENDA: Roy? What's Len saying?

(*ROY refuses to look.*)

Roy.

(*ROY tries to take the jacket off again. IRENE tries to stop him.*)

IRENE: Don't.

BRENDA: God's sake. Leave him alone.

(*BRENDA steps in front of IRENE.*

ROY takes the jacket off.

IRENE backs off.)

BRENDA: (*To ROY.*) Why'd she burn your suit?

LEN: She done it the night Arthur died.

BRENDA: Why?

IRENE: Shut up, Len.

BRENDA: Len?

LEN: You did, Reen.

IRENE: I never done nothing.

ROY: Leave it, Brend. It don't matter.

BRENDA: It does bloody matter. What happened?

LEN: Nothing.

BRENDA: You got to tell me now.

IRENE: He ain't.

LEN: It wasn't nothing.

BRENDA: Len. Look at me. You got to tell me.

(*LEN looks.*)

LEN: I got to?

BRENDA: It's just the truth, what happened, that's all.

LEN: It was after the men took Arthur away in the big car.
Roy was in bed, then he got up and put his suit on and
went out.

BRENDA: Where?

IRENE: Shut up.

BRENDA: No. It's all right, Len. Tell me.

LEN: He went to see Linda.
Reen waited for him to come back then she got hold of
the suit. They had this row, that's when the chairs was all
tipped over.

BRENDA: You sure?

LEN: I heard it. The plates was all smashed then she set fire
to the suit in the fireplace, and said there, that'll stop you
seeing that filthy bitch.

BRENDA: Jesus.

LEN: That's right, ain't it, Roy?

(*No answer.*)

It is right. But she was upset, Brend. About Arthur. Like
I said to her, people get upset and they don't know what
they're doing.

BRENDA: (*To IRENE.*) I told you before, you can't carry on
like that.

LEN: It was just she was upset.

ROY: Leave it, Brend. Not today.

BRENDA: No. I ain't leaving it.
You can't let her get away with it.

ROY: Brend.

(*BRENDA steps towards IRENE.*)

BRENDA: I know what you do. It ain't right.
Sleeping in his bed to catch him out when he comes in.
Are you listening? Writing down the mileage of his car to

56

see where he's been. Picking up his bloody clothes and
smelling them.

ROY: You said all this before.

BRENDA: What am I sposed to do then, say nothing?

ROY: It ain't that.

BRENDA: So what is it?

ROY: You can't speak for me. You got to let me say it.

BRENDA: But you don't.

You don't.

(*Pause.*)

Go on, Roy. Tell her. Tell her she can't do it.

ROY: No.

BRENDA: She's waiting. Tell her.

ROY: Not now.

BRENDA: You know, it was her stopped you. You got to think
about what you've given up cos of her.

You could have had your own family now, Roy. You could
be with Linda. You and Linda and your child.

(*ROY steps forward quickly to stop BRENDA.*)

ROY: That's enough.

BRENDA: It ain't.

ROY: Shut up.

You think I don't know that?

(*BRENDA backs away.*)

BRENDA: I'm only saying what's true.

ROY: (*Shouts.*) Shut up. Just shut up.

(*LINDA enters the orchard.*

*IRENE sees LINDA and gathers the grafting and pruning
knives, takes a step back.*

ROY stares at LINDA and she approaches.)

LINDA: I didn't like to go without saying.

I've done what I can.

BRENDA: Thanks.

LINDA: It's all right. Least I helped with something.

LEN: You're still here.

LINDA: I am, yeh.

LEN: Reen didn't wanna come in. I told her you and Brend
had done a tea, but she said she wasn't coming in while
you was there.

BRENDA: Len.

LEN: It's only what she said.

LINDA: It's all right. I knew, anyway.

Are you all right, Brend?

BRENDA: I'm fine. Just come out to see they were all right.

(*LINDA looks round the orchard.*)

LEN: We ain't seen you out here for a bit.

LINDA: Not for a long time.

LEN: You liked coming when you was a young'n.

(*IRENE straightens up, watches and listens.*)

LINDA: I did, yeh.

LEN: Remember it, do you?

LINDA: Course I do. My mother thought I was gonna move
in at one point, I was here that much.

LEN: You wasn't no trouble.

LINDA: Not then, no. I was only trouble when I grew up,
Len.

Look, I should get on.

(*LINDA moves as if to go. ROY echoes her move.*)

BRENDA: I don't want you to go.

(*LINDA stops.*)

LINDA: I got things I got to do.

BRENDA: Please.

You were here a lot. Out here a lot.

LEN: She was. You seen all the apples, Linda?

LINDA: I have, yeh. Looks like there's loads.

LEN: Been a good year.

LINDA: Good year for apples, good year for twins, that's
right, ain't it?

BRENDA: So they say.

LEN: Yeh. Been a good year.

LINDA: Must've been all that rain then there was the warm
spring.

LEN: That's it. Perfect for them. Perfect for growing.
Perfect, yeh.

BRENDA: We were saying the time we spent out here.

LINDA: Yeh.

BRENDA: Singing the songs.

LINDA: And the bagging up.

What was it? Beauty of Bath, Royal Somerset, Kingston Black.

BRENDA: Yeh.

LINDA: That game, planting the trees. The first people here. First man, first woman, first baby. I hated being the baby.

BRENDA: You were the youngest.

There was all that bottling and pressing, and storing.

LINDA: Yeh.

BRENDA: I kept finding it for years after, jars full of mould and that.

LEN: I liked that game.

LINDA: You did.

(*Looking round.*) You wouldn't know it now.

BRENDA: No.

LINDA: Like a different world.

(*To ROY.*) Roy, you all right?

(*ROY nods.*)

It was a good service.

(*LEN slowly begins picking up apples, placing them in a bag.*)

ROY: Yeh.

LINDA: Lot of people, considering his age.

ROY: Yeh.

LINDA: Glad I came.

BRENDA: Good.

LINDA: And he did a good job, the vicar.

This morning, before I left home, I was thinking, all that time up the trees, with the press.

Brought back so many things, coming back.

There was that time, Roy, when you ate an apple, and swallowed the pip. You thought it'd grow in your belly. You were saying you thought the branches'd run along your arms, down your legs.

ROY: Oh yeh. (*Laughs.*)

LINDA: Crying, you were.

ROY: Thought I'd have a mouth full of fruit.

LINDA: Did you?

ROY: An apple on my tongue. Stopping me breathing.

LINDA: Where d'you get that from?

ROY: Dunno. I could've spat it out anyway.

LINDA: Or swallowed.

ROY: It was a bloody big apple.

LINDA: You were a daft sod.

ROY: Yeh.

LINDA: Near as soft as your father. It was you a lot of the time, making us run round, doing all that with the apples.

ROY: You loved it.

LINDA: I did, yeh.

ROY: Thanks for coming.

LINDA: You asked me.

IRENE: Look at her.

BRENDA: Leave her.

IRENE: Look. She's standing here sizing it all up. Working out how to get her hands on it. Only you lot can't see it.

BRENDA: Mother.

IRENE: There's nothing here for you. You wanna get back to where you're from.

ROY: Stop it.

IRENE: Stop what?

(*IRENE turns away and watches LEN. Listens.*)

ROY: Take no notice. She ain't been well.

LINDA: I'm sure she hasn't. Look, I'll go. It's easiest.

(*LINDA goes to leave. BRENDA pulls her arm.*)

BRENDA: (*Sharp.*) Don't.

LINDA: How could she say that?

I loved it out here.

BRENDA: Course you did.

ROY: Don't listen to it.

(*LINDA makes a move to go.*)

BRENDA: (*Quick.*) It's been a long time. You should've come back before.

LINDA: Don't say that.

BRENDA: You should. Shouldn't she, Roy.

ROY: (*Sharp.*) Leave it.

BRENDA: No. I ain't gonna leave it.

You're doing it again. You're gonna let her just go.

LINDA: Brend. Please don't.

    (*IRENE cries out, staggers.*)

IRENE: I didn't get any sleep.

    No I didn't get no sleep.

    I was awake all night and there was a weight on the
mattress, a voice in the room.

    I think –

    I think I have a head full of leaves. A skull full of blossom.

    I got the orchard in my head.

    (*Pause.*)

ROY: Christ.

    You all right?

IRENE: No.

    No. I'm not.

    (*BRENDA steps towards IRENE. IRENE backs away.*)

    Don't touch me.

    (*LINDA moves forward.*)

    Don't come near me.

ROY: It's all right.

IRENE: Is that you, Roy?

    (*ROY steps forward.*)

ROY: It's me, yeh.

    (*IRENE reaches out and holds ROY's hand.*)

IRENE: Roy.

ROY: Yeh.

IRENE: I did swallow the pips.

ROY: Course you did.

IRENE: I rubbed the apple skin till the devil jumped out.

ROY: You did.

IRENE: But did I do enough?

ROY: You did, yeh.

    You'll be all right now.

IRENE: Will I?

ROY: Yeh.

    (*IRENE stands, a child, her hand in ROY's. LEN moves
closer.*)

BRENDA: Roy.

    Every time anyone says summat, she does this.

    Can't you see?

ROY: She ain't well.

BRENDA: Then get the doctor in.

(No response.)

Go on. Call the doctor.

LINDA: Brenda, leave it.

ROY: She'll be fine in a minute.

BRENDA: I'm sure she will.

We'll talk about how it's getting cold and dark and what a good autumn it's been and she'll be fine.

LEN: *(Fearful.)* I don't know what's happening any more.

BRENDA: It's all right.

LEN: What's going on, Brend?

BRENDA: Nothing.

LEN: It is getting dark. And cold.

BRENDA: Yeh. It is.

LEN: And there's a lot of apples, Brend.

(No response.)

I said there's a lot of apples.

BRENDA: There is.

LEN: Been a good autumn.

BRENDA: It has, yeh.

(Pause.)

Roy. Let go.

ROY: What?

BRENDA: Let go.

(ROY lets go of IRENE's hand.)

LINDA: I'm gonna go now, Roy.

ROY: Right.

BRENDA: You gonna let her?

LINDA: Brend. Don't.

BRENDA: Why?

(Gesturing at IRENE.) You can't let her do this to you.

He can't, can he, Linda?

LINDA: Don't, Brend.

BRENDA: Come on, Linda.

LINDA: *(Cries out.)* No. Stop it.

BRENDA: What?

LINDA: Nothing.

BRENDA: What is it?

LINDA: (*To ROY, gestures at IRENE.*) You'd better take her off.
Go and help Len.

ROY: Why?

LINDA: Cos I'm asking you to.

ROY: I don't understand.

LINDA: Look, just go and do the bagging. Please.

ROY: If that's what you want.

LINDA: It is.

(*ROY takes IRENE's arm and walks away with LEN.
Silence.*)

LINDA: I won't be used as a weapon.

BRENDA: No.

I'm sorry.

LINDA: Look, I'm glad I went to the church but I should
never've come back here. I've made a stupid mistake.

BRENDA: No. You haven't.

He came to you when Father died. To you.

LINDA: Only because he knew where I was. And because he
knew how I felt about your dad.

BRENDA: You know it's not just that. He wanted you.

LINDA: No.

Oh, Brenda.

It would never have worked out, not while she's here, not
while the farm's here.

BRENDA: It ain't too late. It's changed now Father's died.
They can't stay here and do nothing. The bank's started
on at them. There's all this land to be sold for building.
They'll have to do it to pay off the debts.

(*No response.*)

Linda. I had the row about all that with you and Roy, and
I didn't come here for three years. Didn't come and see
Father.

And now it's too late.

LINDA: But it's too late for me too.

BRENDA: (*Realises.*) Have you got someone else?

LINDA: Brenda, I have to go.

BRENDA: You have.

(*LINDA nods.*)

I see.

LINDA: He was in the house when Roy came round, but he was in bed, so Roy didn't see him.

BRENDA: Is it serious?

LINDA: I'm pregnant.

(*Pause.*)

It was my last chance.

BRENDA: Does Roy know?

LINDA: I couldn't tell him. Your dad'd just died.

BRENDA: But he knows you got someone else?

LINDA: I couldn't tell him.

(*Pause.*)

BRENDA: How many months?

LINDA: Four.

BRENDA: Are you happy?

Sorry. I shouldn't.

LINDA: It's okay.

I'm looking forward to the baby.

BRENDA: I see.

(*Pause.*)

Linda.

I got to ask you.

If you'd kept Roy's baby back then, what would have happened?

(*LINDA hesitates.*)

LINDA: I wonder sometimes.

Let myself think if I'd just carried on, had the baby. Maybe he'd have come to see us and maybe that would have given him the strength to leave here and come to us.

BRENDA: Maybe he would have.

LINDA: But he wouldn't. You know that. (*Angry.*) Nothing would have changed. He'd have made excuses, kept coming back here.

I didn't believe him any more.

He could have had us, Brend.

BRENDA: She stopped him. It was her.

LINDA: Look, I appreciate it. You know, what you did then.

BRENDA: But it made no difference.

LINDA: That's not true. It did to me. That you'd be that angry, that you'd make such a stand for me. And for the baby.

BRENDA: But it made no difference.

LINDA: I would have been there on my own with the baby, waiting for him to come. And I would have been hurt over and over and over.

I just couldn't go through with it. I'm really sorry.

BRENDA: You don't have to say sorry.

LINDA: But I want to. It's being back here, thinking of your dad.

Realising the baby was part of your family.

BRENDA: It's all right.

LINDA: I really did love Roy.

BRENDA: I know.

(*Pause.*)

LINDA: I still love him.

(*Pause.*)

I waited a long time for him. I waited more than twenty years.

D'you understand?

BRENDA: Of course I do.

I'd have done anything for a child.

Shit. I don't mean. I'm not trying to say anything.

LINDA: I know.

BRENDA: About you getting rid of it.

I just mean I'd have done anything to have a baby. For me. I know what that feels like.

LINDA: Brenda. I know what you mean.

(*Pause.*)

Look, I think it's best if I go.

(*LINDA goes to leave.*)

BRENDA: Linda.

(*LINDA stops.*)

I saw Dad just the once. After the row. I was behind him in the bank in town.

He didn't know what to say. I asked him how he was. How the farm was. How Roy was.

I asked him if he'd come and see me, but I never heard from him.

LINDA: He couldn't stand up to her.

BRENDA: Why?

LINDA: He just couldn't.

BRENDA: No.

But now I think why didn't I just turn up? Come and see him.

LINDA: Don't be too hard on yourself.

BRENDA: No.

He would've liked it if you'd ended up here, you know that?

LINDA: I do know that, yeh. I do.

(*Pause.*)

Brenda. She's a strong woman.

(*BRENDA nods, can't speak.*)

Oh, Brenda.

(*LINDA steps towards her, but BRENDA steps back, puts her hands up.*)

BRENDA: No.

LINDA: You all right?

(*BRENDA nods. LINDA waits while BRENDA regains control.*)

Okay?

BRENDA: Yeh.

LINDA: Sure?

(*BRENDA nods.*)

I promised I'd get back. I get tired. I've been really sick.

BRENDA: Course.

LINDA: I'm really sorry about your dad. He was a good man.

BRENDA: Thanks.

LINDA: Maybe I'll see you. Maybe –

Would you come and see the baby?

(*No answer.*)

That was such a stupid thing to say. I'm sorry.

(*BRENDA shrugs.*)

BRENDA: It's okay.

LINDA: No. It's not. It's all so…

(*Looking round.*) I want you to know, Brend, I was so happy here. With you too.

(*LINDA looks at BRENDA and leaves, stopping to pick up an apple on her way.*

BRENDA watches her leave, as does ROY.

ROY puts another apple in his bag then returns to BRENDA, bringing the bag.)

ROY: Where's she gone?

She gone in the house?

BRENDA: No.

ROY: She gone home?

BRENDA: Think so.

ROY: Why? What happened?

BRENDA: Nothing.

ROY: Brend.

What happened?

BRENDA: She said before she had to get going.

ROY: But she didn't say nothing to me.

BRENDA: No.

(*ROY goes to move.*)

ROY: I'll see if I can catch her.

BRENDA: No.

ROY: Why? What is it?

BRENDA: It's just it's late. We ought to go in. And you ought to be here, just for today.

ROY: What is it?

BRENDA: Nothing.

Jack'll be home soon. He'll be asking himself where I am.

ROY: But what is it?

BRENDA: Nothing. It's just caught up with me. Today and that.

ROY: Brenda.

(*ROY picks up one of the knives from the ground and runs his finger along the blade.*)

What you said to me before, about what I want.

BRENDA: I didn't mean it. It's just what with all this today.

You got to remember I didn't see Father for all this time.

I've got feelings about that, it's made me say things I didn't mean.

ROY: What is it? Where's Linda gone?

Did she go back home?

BRENDA: She must have.

She –

(*Pause, but BRENDA can't say it.*)

ROY: What?

(*BRENDA shakes her head.*)

BRENDA: Nothing.

Roy.

ROY: What?

BRENDA: I'm gonna come back tomorrow. To give a hand.

(*ROY shrugs.*)

ROY: If you want.

But I don't understand.

(*IRENE moves nearer.*)

I should've gone after her.

BRENDA: Not now. I want you here.

ROY: What is it, Brend?

(*Pause.*)

BRENDA: It's just today.

(*IRENE returns. LEN continues to bag. BRENDA turns away from IRENE and ROY.*)

IRENE: Gone, has she?

ROY: Who?

IRENE: That bloody woman.

ROY: She's gone, yeh.

IRENE: Good. No need for her here.

So we can get on now. Get the apples in.

There's Burrow Hill Early, Ellis Bitter, Court Royal.

Got to get them all in.

ROY: No.

IRENE: Poor Man's Profit, Sweet Coppin.

ROY: I ain't gonna.

IRENE: What you say?

ROY: I ain't gonna.

IRENE: We got to get them in.

ROY: Why?

IRENE: It's what you do.

ROY: What? Get them in to rot?

IRENE: Ain't gonna rot. Gonna get the press cleaned out.

ROY: Are you?

IRENE: Roy.

ROY: When d'we last use the press?

IRENE: What d'you mean?

ROY: The press ain't been used.

IRENE: It has.

ROY: Each year we got the apples in, and each spring I've had to throw them out.

IRENE: What you saying?

ROY: What d'you think I'm saying?

(*Pause.*)

IRENE: Was it the funeral today?

(*No response.*)

I keep remembering this bowl Father made from the apple wood. Mother filled it with roasted apples.

And we'd sing.

(*Sings.*) Oh lily white lily your lily white pin.

Please to come out and let us come in.

I'm tired. I don't think I slept very well.

ROY: Go and lie down, then.

(*Pause.*)

IRENE: (*To ROY.*) She's still here.

ROY: She is, yeh.

IRENE: You gonna tell her to go? Let us get back to normal.

ROY: No.

BRENDA: Roy. Don't.

ROY: (*To IRENE.*) No I ain't.

IRENE: We don't need her.

ROY: No?

IRENE: Ain't nothing wrong here. We'll manage, long as I got you.

ROY: But you ain't.

IRENE: What?

ROY: I said you ain't.

(*BRENDA shakes her head, places her head in her hands.*)

IRENE: I don't know what you're saying. It's the shock of it and what's happened. No-one knows what they're saying.

ROY: They do. They know exactly what they're saying.

IRENE: But I didn't get no sleep. I'm tired.

ROY: Are you?

IRENE: The birds've gone quiet.

And I'm cold.

ROY: Yeh?

(*BRENDA looks up.*)

BRENDA: Leave it now, Roy. Stay here today.

ROY: No. I'm gonna go.

IRENE: Gonna go, are you?

ROY: That's what I said.

IRENE: I don't believe you.

(*Waits.*)

Look at you. You ain't moving.

Go on. I've had enough.

Fuck off and go.

ROY: You saying that to me?

IRENE: I am, yeh.

Go on.

ROY: So I'm gonna go.

IRENE: You still ain't moving.

(*ROY takes a step.*)

ROY: There.

IRENE: Go on. Another.

BRENDA: Roy. Don't.

ROY: Why?

BRENDA: Not today.

Please.

ROY: But you wanted me to go. You wanted this.

BRENDA: No.

ROY: But she'll be waiting for me, Brend.

(*BRENDA watches as ROY walks to his apple bag.
ROY tips the apples from his bag on the ground and they roll
and scatter.*)

ROY *throws the hessian bag and leaves.*
IRENE *watches him go.*
Silence while the apples roll and come to rest.)
IRENE: Where's he gone?
BRENDA: You know where he's gone.
IRENE: He's gone to see Linda.
(*IRENE looks away.*)
BRENDA: He thinks she's waiting for him.
IRENE: Will he stay there?
BRENDA: No.
IRENE: Why?
(*No response.*)
Why?
BRENDA: You want me to tell you why?
IRENE: I do, yeh.
BRENDA: You do. Right.
He won't stay because when he goes down there thinking
she's waiting for him…
(*IRENE looks away, takes a step. BRENDA grabs her arm,
pulls her back.*)
No. You said you wanted to know. Now you got to listen.
When he goes down she's gonna let him in.
(*IRENE looks away but BRENDA pulls her face round, forces
her to look.*)
Listen to me.
And she's gonna have to say it.
That he's too late.
That even though she still loves him, she has another
man's baby inside her.
How's that make you feel?
IRENE: She's a filthy fucking bitch.
(*BRENDA slaps IRENE.*)
BRENDA: My God. I didn't mean to do that.
I'm sorry.
(*Pause.*)
I'm sorry. I shouldn't have done that.
You all right?

IRENE: No.

    I got this feeling.

    (*IRENE touches her belly.*)

    Got a belly full of leaves.

BRENDA: Have you?

IRENE: Got a skull full of blossom.

BRENDA: Have you?

IRENE: Was it the funeral today?

BRENDA: You know it was.

    Don't start that. Not with me.

IRENE: No. Not with you.

BRENDA: Look at me.

    (*No response.*)

    I said look.

    (*IRENE looks directly at BRENDA.*)

    You know what you've done?

IRENE: It was you done it. You coming back.

BRENDA: You can't blame me.

IRENE: It was all right before you come back.

    Why don't you go back home.

BRENDA: I am home.

    (*Pause.*)

    I am home.

    (*Pause.*)

IRENE: Will he come back?

BRENDA: I don't know.

IRENE: But there's all the apples.

BRENDA: I know.

IRENE: The day my mother died, my eyes got red and sore
    and it wouldn't go.

    Father made me lie down on my back, still, and he put
    linen over my eyes. He laid down a poultice from rotten
    apples. Put an apple pip between my teeth.

    I lay there for a while, biting down on the pip. Then he
    took it off.

    I stood and opened my eyes.

    I could see. But my world wasn't the same and it never was
    again.

BRENDA: How old were you?

IRENE: Young.

BRENDA: How long was she ill?

IRENE: Why you asking?

BRENDA: I want to know.

IRENE: Not long. She was in her room a bit then we never
saw her again.

It was me, Len and Father. Till I met Arthur.

(*Pause.*)

When I met him I threw an apple pip in the fire, said his
name.

If you love me, I said, pop and fly, if you hate me lay and
die.

The pip flew right out across the room and we was married
within the month.

The night we wed, he put the apple under the bolster.

Then we had children. A son. Roy.

BRENDA: And me. You had me.

IRENE: You should've had children.

BRENDA: Well I didn't.

(*Snaps.*) I couldn't.

IRENE: You should've had a son.

BRENDA: You know I couldn't.

Mother, you know something?

You don't have to hurt me.

It doesn't have to be like that.

(*IRENE looks at her and they hold their look.*)

Why was it Roy?

(*No answer.*)

All that you did for him, and you did nothing for me.

(*IRENE looks away.*)

Why?

IRENE: You didn't need me.

BRENDA: I did.

IRENE: No. Women manage.

BRENDA: No. You managed.

(*Silence.*

BRENDA steps closer.)

You must be tired. It's been a long day.

Let me take you in.

(*IRENE moves back slightly.*)

IRENE: No.

BRENDA: Why not?

IRENE: Don't want you to.

I don't want you here.

BRENDA: I know you don't.

IRENE: I didn't want a daughter.

BRENDA: But you got one.

(*Pause.*)

IRENE: Will he come back?

BRENDA: I don't know.

IRENE: You know, as a girl I was told, don't bring the blossom in the house. Father it was, said it.

But after I married, I went out in the orchard with Arthur, and we was working with the trees, and I picked some of the blossom, looked at it.

I wandered back through the orchard, through the home field, into the house. I looked down and saw it was still there in my hand. And it was too late. I'd brought the bad luck in.

BRENDA: This ain't to do with luck.

(*Pause.*)

IRENE: No.

BRENDA: You did this.

IRENE: I know I did.

(*Pause.*)

BRENDA: You know you'll lose all this if you do nothing.

You want to lose it?

IRENE: No.

I do know the state it's in. I know it's going.

BRENDA: Mum.

IRENE: But it's all I got.

It's all I got and I don't want to be here to see it gone.

I don't want houses here. Don't want lights in the fields.

I don't want other people here walking on this ground.

BRENDA: No. I know.

IRENE: And there's nothing you can say.

BRENDA: No. There isn't.

(*Pause.*

IRENE takes the spade and starts to dig the hole with it.)

BRENDA: What you doing?

(*No answer.*)

Let me.

Let me help you.

(*IRENE looks at BRENDA, passes her the spade. BRENDA digs while IRENE watches.*)

IRENE: That's enough.

(*IRENE places the grafting knives in the hole, covers them.*)

BRENDA: Is there anything else you need me to do?

IRENE: Yes.

BRENDA: Good. I'll do anything for you.

IRENE: Why?

BRENDA: Because you're my mother.

IRENE: And you are my daughter.

BRENDA: I am.

IRENE: There is something else.

(*BRENDA waits.*)

I just want to be here quiet.

BRENDA: Don't tell me to go.

IRENE: I want you to.

BRENDA: No.

IRENE: You said you'd do anything.

BRENDA: If that's what you really want.

IRENE: It is.

BRENDA: Right.

Right.

(*BRENDA waits, then nods and leaves.*

IRENE does not watch BRENDA go, but finishes covering the knives.

The light is fading fast.

LEN returns with the bag of apples.

Silence, then:)

LEN: It's late. Getting dark.

(*Pause.*)

IRENE: It is.

    You get a sky this clear, you know it's gonna get cold.

LEN: I'll need my coat.

IRENE: You will, yeh.

LEN: Thing is, with the winter, it's the bare branches.

    Shape of them gets stuck in my head.

    And the birds fall quiet.

IRENE: Fall quiet, yeh.

    (*Pause.*)

    You bagged the apples, then.

LEN: I did.

    Foxwhelp.

IRENE: Blood Butcher.

LEN: Pennard Bitter.

IRENE: Neverblight.

    (*IRENE looks up at the sky, LEN copies.*)

LEN: Sometimes the sky feels heavy.

IRENE: Does it?

LEN: And sometimes the dark gets in my head.

    Gets so I'm cold inside.

IRENE: Does it?

LEN: Like I said, I don't like autumn.

    It's the dark evenings. And the leaves dying I don't like.

    (*No response.*)

    Reen.

IRENE: What?

LEN: Reen.

IRENE: What?

LEN: We don't know what's gonna happen, do us?

IRENE: No.

LEN: We will be all right, won't we?

IRENE: What d'you want me to say?

LEN: That we'll be all right.

IRENE: Do you?

LEN: Say it.

IRENE: No.

    (*Pause.*)

LEN: Reen.

IRENE: What?

LEN: Do me the story of the orchard.

IRENE: I don't know it.

LEN: Course you do.

IRENE: I don't.

LEN: Reen.

(No response.)

You do.

IRENE: I know.

LEN: You tell it now, Reen?

IRENE: Not now. I can't

LEN: Please, Reen.

IRENE: I can't, not like before.

LEN: Do it like you can.

(During the story IRENE slowly undresses LEN, taking off his shoes and socks, then jacket, folding them neatly on the ground.)

IRENE: The Apple Tree Man climbs down from the oldest branches and stands on the grass.

He listens as all the apples fall down onto the grass, the sound like rolling thunder. The leaves go red then brown and curl and die. Fall to the ground.

The roots begin to dry out and then the branches die.

The Apple Tree Man falls to his knees and crawls through the room of dead trees till he finds the woman. He crawls up her open thighs, and he pushes himself back into the dark space right inside of her.

LEN: Has he gone back in?

IRENE: He has, yeh. He's slipped back between her legs.

LEN: What's he got in his arms?

IRENE: He's got the diseases. Silver leaf. Scab.

LEN: Codling Moth.

IRENE: Canker.

And the woman and the man stand there on the grass.

LEN: Stand there.

IRENE: The weight of the sky presses down on them, presses the apples on the grass, presses the dead leaves, the roots and branches, deep down into the soil.

LEN: Beauty of Bath.

IRENE: Kingston Black.

LEN: Royal Somerset.

IRENE: The soil is red and wet and the man and woman slip down through the crust of the earth.

Their skin red and wet.

The earth closes over them, and there's no sign they ever been there.

And the snow falls and covers the earth and the stars move away and the sun dies.

And it's cold and the dark.

And the world is cold and dark and flat.

Just as it was at the beginning.

(*Leaves begin to fall.*

LEN is in his vest and trousers and bare feet. He lies down.

IRENE covers LEN with leaves.

IRENE looks up at the black sky and sings:)

We know by the moon that we are not too soon

And we know by the sky that we are not too high

We know by the star that we are not too far

And we know by the ground that we are within sound.

(*IRENE takes off her coat and dress and boots. She lies down next to LEN and covers herself with leaves.*

The last leaves fall and the last light fades.)

www.ingramcontent.com/pod-product-compliance
Ingram Content Group UK Ltd.
Pitfield, Milton Keynes, MK11 3LW, UK
UKHW020739280225
455688UK00013B/746